D0882934

Like the Iris of an Eye

Susan Griffin

LIKE THE

✓76 – 9193

RIS OF AN EYE.

451022

811
G852L

HARPER & ROW, PUBLISHERS

New York, Hagerstown, San Francisco, London

East Baton Rouge Parish Library
Baton Rouge, Louisiana

Grateful acknowledgment is made to the publishers of the follow-
ing books and magazines in which some of the poems have ap-
peared:

BOOKS: *Amazon Poetry* (Out and Out Books); *Anthology of
Women Poets* (Dremen Press); *Dear Sky* (Shameless Hussy
Press); *Lesbian Reader* (Amazon Press); *Let Them Be Said*
(Mama's Press); *Mountain Moving Day* (Crossing Press); *The
New Woman's Survival Sourcebook* (Alfred A. Knopf and Co.);
No More Masks (Doubleday and Co.); *Rising Tides* (Washington
Square Press); *This Is Woman's Work* (Panjandram Press);
What Woman, and Who, Myself, I Am (Wooden Shoe Press)

MAGAZINES: *Aldebaran Review*; *Amazon Quarterly*; *Big Moon*;
Country Women; *Everywoman*; *It Ain't Me, Babe*; *Mosaic*; *Ms.*;
New; *Plexus*; *Room*; *Shocks*

LIKE THE IRIS OF AN EYE. Copyright © 1976 by Susan Griffin.
All rights reserved. Printed in the United States of America. No
part of this book may be used or reproduced in any manner what-
soever without written permission except in the case of brief quota-
tions embodied in critical articles and reviews. For information
address Harper & Row, Publishers, Inc., 10 East 53rd Street, New
York, N.Y. 10022. Published simultaneously in Canada by Fitz-
henry & Whiteside Limited, Toronto.

FIRST EDITION

Designed by Dorothy Schmiderer

Library of Congress Cataloging in Publication Data
Griffin, Susan.
  Like the iris of an eye.
  I. Title.
PS3557.R48913A17   1976   811'.5'4   76-9193
ISBN 0-06-011513-0

---

76 77 78 79 80 10 9 8 7 6 5 4 3 2 1

For Emily I. Colvin and Nelle U. Branch—two sisters, my grandmother and my great aunt, and the lives they lived, the one working in her home, raising her own child, and then a grandchild, teaching her to read; the other a teacher, a librarian, raising her niece's child— for their early hours, their strength, for the love between them, and for all that was not said, for all that was stifled and bitter in them, in anger and in love, these poems

Acknowledgments

I would like to thank Pat Dientsfry, Nancy Stockwell and Gloria Bowles for their generous help in the preparation of this manuscript; Adrienne Rich for her reading and her nurturing of these poems, in ways too deep to list; Fran McCullough for her intelligent and sensitive editing, and Betsy Groban for her careful work; Thalia Kitrilakis for her friendship to me and to these poems. And I am also deeply grateful to Kay Boyle, Josephine Miles and Tillie Olsen with whom I have studied and learned, for continuing support and especially for their words.

Contents

III THE TIREDNESS CYCLE
(1973–1974)

IV NEW POEMS (1973–1976)

I

EARLY POEMS

(1967–1973)

from DEAR SKY *and* LET THEM BE SAID

Love Should Grow Up Like a Wild Iris in the Fields

Love should grow up like a wild iris in the fields,
unexpected, after a terrible storm, opening a purple
mouth to the rain, with not a thought to the future,
ignorant of the grass and the graveyard of leaves
around, forgetting its own beginning. Love should
grow like a wild iris
but does not.
Love more often is to be found in kitchens at the dinner
      hour,
tired out and hungry, lingers over tables in houses where
the walls record movements; while the cook is probably
      angry,
and the ingredients of the meal are budgeted, while
a child cries feed me now and her mother not quite
hysterical says over and over, wait just a bit, just a bit,
love should grow up in the fields like a wild iris
but never does
really startle anyone, was to be expected, was to be
predicted, is almost absurd, goes on from day to day, not
      quite
blindly, gets taken to the cleaners every fall, sings old
songs over and over, and falls on the same piece of rug
      that
never gets tacked down, gives up, wants to hide, is not
brave, knows too much, is not like an
iris growing wild but more like
staring into space
in the street
not quite sure

which door it was, annoyed about the sidewalk being
slippery, trying all the doors, thinking
if love wished the world to be well, it would be well.
Love should
grow up like a wild iris, but doesn't, it comes from
the midst of everything else, sees like the iris
of an eye, when the light is right,
feels in blindness and when there is nothing else is
tender, blinks, and opens
face up to the skies.

The Woman

The woman
with teeth like a horse
moves swiftly
her jaw silhouetted against
life the carriage, a
passing
green curve
the fall bushes
shiver in the
mild white sun, a face
passing over the face of the earth,
a young colt
is reflected in her teeth
his tendons gleaming we are
growing old
and hold
each smell inside
and see the sky through
the smell of your sperm
and our sweat, one could die
to look at your long
irregular toes
we sitting on the ground
your hand
in the wetness
between my arm and my
breast, the wet, the
bush, your white shirt
smiles at me
saying this is a

moment, now, right now
a terrible moment
a colt is being born
in my mind covered with
his mother's blood
she licks off
in my skull
the old horse
hooves sticky
limps among weeds
your shirt
smiles at me
and I feel
my heart
pumping
blood and
turning
my face red.

Revolution

I would not have gotten in this boat with you.
I would not
except
where else was there
at the dock's end
to go?
The water
was cold.

I would not have let you row the boat.
I could see
what kind of man you were.
I would not but
who was there to choose
between
you and me?

I would not have let you throw away the oars.
I knew what would happen next,
except
what else was there to do,
struggle
in a boat with a leak
over cold water?

To Gather Ourselves

This is thanks
giving a day to
gather ourselves; I
have gathered myself
this morning with
two cups of coffee
watching my daughter play
pots and pans on the kitchen floor. I
don't worry about the time.
I watch the sky clear, and
I read poems about the war
which have been
waiting on my shelf
for one year.
The war escalated again just
yesterday, and I
have been busy all week
trying to research
how many rapes took place
at My Lai?
Every interruption leads us
in the same direction, there
can be no
stopping us from being
what we are,
sleep leads to dreaming
waking to imagination and to
imagine what we
could be, O,
what we could be.

Is *the Air Political Today?*

Is the air political today?
The air, my thoughts,
is this a
political hour? did you
choose a political chair
to sit in; was
my logic political, were my
eyes, did they
show a political grief or
was it personal; would my political
self have been happy
when I was not; would they
have fought over me
struggling over the tongue; is my tongue
political when it rests still
between my teeth and I dream;
what was birth
the placenta that was pulled from me
was that political?
I cannot
shut myself up
anywhere; is that
a political feeling? Are you
more political than I, tonight,
or were you this morning and tell
me now
in which journal shall I write
that I miss my child
and want to hold
her, let her political
head rest between my
political breast and shoulder?

I Like to Think of Harriet Tubman

I like to think of Harriet Tubman.
Harriet Tubman who carried a revolver,
who had a scar on her head from a rock thrown
by a slave-master (because she
talked back), and who
had a ransom on her head
of thousands of dollars and who
was never caught, and who
had no use for the law
when the law was wrong,
who defied the law. I like
to think of her.
I like to think of her especially
when I think of the problem of
feeding children.

The legal answer
to the problem of feeding children
is ten free lunches every month,
being equal, in the child's real life,
to eating lunch every other day.
Monday but not Tuesday.
I like to think of the President
eating lunch Monday, but not
Tuesday.
And when I think of the President
and the law, and the problem of
feeding children, I like to
think of Harriet Tubman
and her revolver.

And then sometimes
I think of the President
and other men,
men who practice the law,
who revere the law,
who make the law,
who enforce the law,
who live behind
and operate through
and feed themselves
at the expense of
starving children
because of the law.

Men who sit in paneled offices
and think about vacations
and tell women
whose care it is
to feed children
not to be hysterical
not to be hysterical as in the word
hysterikos, the greek for
womb suffering,
not to suffer in their
wombs,
not to care,
not to bother the men
because they want to think
of other things
and do not want
to take the women seriously.
I want them
to take women seriously.

I want them to think about Harriet Tubman,
and remember,
remember she was beat by a white man
and she lived
and she lived to redress her grievances,
and she lived in swamps
and wore the clothes of a man
bringing hundreds of fugitives from
slavery, and was never caught,
and led an army,
and won a battle,
and defied the laws
because the laws were wrong, I want men
to take us seriously.
I am tired wanting them to think
about right and wrong.
I want them to fear.
I want them to feel fear now
as I have felt suffering in the womb, and
I want them
to know
that there is always a time
there is always a time to make right
what is wrong,
there is always a time
for retribution
and that time
is beginning.

Three Poems for Women

1

This is a poem for a woman doing dishes.
This is a poem for a woman doing dishes.
It must be repeated.
It must be repeated,
again and again,
again and again,
because the woman doing dishes
because the woman doing dishes
has trouble hearing
has trouble hearing.

2

And this is another poem for a woman
cleaning the floor
who cannot hear at all.
Let us have a moment of silence
for the woman who cleans the floor.

3

And here is one more poem
for the woman at home
with children.
You never see her at night.
Stare at an empty space and imagine her there,
the woman with children
because she cannot be here to speak
for herself,
and listen
to what you think
she might say.

In My Dream

I woke up
this morning in your arms
and drove directly
into the water; it was
storming a few days before
spring, I thought I would
drown.   Now,
sunlight fills my body,
swims behind my eyes.
I have traveled miles
in circles; I am still
in California, after months
in treacherous wet jungles,
after my ship went adrift,
several trains crashed in the night,
cars turned over.
I hitched and did not get a
ride for three weeks in the
Mojave desert, in the winter,
my daughter and I slept
curled together by the side of the road,
my thumb frozen west.
I am still in California
in a public park
but no one around me sees
that in my head
I am resting exhausted
on top of a mesa,
some mesa where the Navajo dwell,
artists of dryness,

doing paintings with sand. I
feel ancient, and each
flicker of my eye-
lids makes me young
again. Do these Navajos here
(I hear the sound of mothers
with children in the sand
surrounding me)
do they lie against one another
in this warmth, put their
faces into lovers' armpits,
lay their cheeks on bellies,
let the fluid of their bodies
flow together?
I have not loved in
so long, I imagine
I have never loved
the way these
Navajos in my mind
can love. This morning,
years ago,
when I woke up
in your arms, I was
in New England, had visited
the home of Emily Dickinson,
was traveling by coach
to Manhattan; the rain on
the leather roof steady,
the dark horse hooves
treading through rock
and mud, my mind sharp
and keen as the iris
in her eye, the poet

who said, the
soul is its own
lonely companion.
I have not seen you since you
left your marriage
leaving me in mine,
wondering what pain in you
drove you half wild
and to the East Coast.
I woke to rainfall and
your absence, sudden
as your being
which surprised me in
a dream.
(Now I hold the glittering
pieces of it
as sunlight dries the rain.)
I drove into the rain-
fall just to find you
again, as I had dreamed,
standing among a party
of my friends.
I was shocked
you saw
I was going down
and touching me
my sorrow
rushed into you.
You had such wildness
when you left you nearly died
and that's what I wanted driving
on rain-wet curves.
We left marriage

and found ourselves
full of love; I thought
I would drown in it, now
sunlight
fills my body
in a park
where I walk
holding my daughter's hand,
she has played in the sand
and the grains on my skin
are turning hard and crystal
in the dark night of
dreams.

She Was Twenty-Three

I was nineteen,
she had slashed her wrists
and tried other things.
She was blond and thin, and
wandered about places
looking at the floor.
I had known her husband, and
I had seen her once before,
before the wrists.
She was bright and quick then,
still I liked her better
after. I met her once
in a hallway moving
from apartment to apartment
and have not seen her since.
I need to know now
is she still
alive and how.

White Bear

In 1867
White Bear
a Kiowa Indian
known for his courage
and eloquence
said to the United
States Congress,

*"I have heard that you intend to
settle us on a reservation near the
mountains. I don't want to settle.
I love to roam over the prairies.
There I feel free and happy, but
when we settle down we grow
pale and die."*

I read this in a museum
White Bear's medicine bag behind
a glass case and me
on the other side
thinking, it is clear
I do not know how to live
anymore words do not
even come to my mouth,
I want to
forget all I have
learned
if it has
led to this, these
Indians knew how to

ride ponies at age five,
chew porcupine needles,
use river clay and plant dyes,
and I tell you,
they had beautiful songs to sing.

I press my hand to the glass
and read
White Bear
committed suicide
in a prison
in Huntsville Texas, 1878. What
reward is there
for patience, I slide my
hand on the cool glass
the keeper lets me through the door.
What shall I do now?
I ask, pedaling my bicycle
up the street.

At home
my daughter waits,
the innocent jailor,
together
we grow pale
doing dishes
and answering the telephone.
She runs
twice as much
as I, yells
much louder,
and when she's unhappy
she cries.

I teach her
to beware of
electricity and
fire.
What else she learns,
I am afraid to
name.

Chance Meeting

This is how it happens.
I am walking away
from the bookstore,
my head reeling with
images of bear cubs their
fur glistening
with dew (disappearing
from the poet's glance
into forests) and my mouth full
of the poet's words against the
rich who
DO NOT HEAR WEEPING.
I wonder at the strangers
walking the pavement and
want to go deep
into a foreign country
where poverty is visible
and no bones are made
about pain,
when I see
(in the window of a shop)
a sign reading "closed" and
know I am late,
move swiftly thinking of
dinner and zucchini plants
and a dog that
needs to run free and you
I want to be with, then
suddenly
there is a mistake,

                  my car
appears
in the middle of the block,
it carries my daughter
with her father
and his new woman
they are going
to a restaurant.

I slip quickly
down
the street
so she won't see
me, my daughter, there should be
no tears, a
pleasant dinner.

My daughter, my heart cleaves
at this, when I see
you, I want to
touch your face, window, glass,
SIDEWALK, STRANGERS,
CARS, DO YOU KNOW,
I fed this child
through the night
whom now
I run from.

Daughter

I look
carefully around the
door to see
your face sweet
like a child in a dream
you sleep.
What are
you
dreaming
in your child's mind?
You spent the last hour
of your day
in misery,
toes and knees that hurt,
dolls falling over,
bottles empty;
tears invaded your
cheeks while
over and over
you tossed the blankets off
pleading, "Cover me."
What's making you cry?
I wanted to know
and held you
as you climbed away
as I sighed,
I'm tired,
let me rest,
go to sleep, my daughter.

The Snow

Black covers their
heads so young
in mourning the
village women of
the old life
going back and forth with
water and fire
wood, day upon day hard
against land that does not
yield or sea that
swallows, and sometimes
lying down, they lift
their black skirts,
worn for the first
Grandfather dead or still
born child, and
press a squalling
and a breathing out
with no apology
for disrupting
the funerals, but rocking and wet,
press the creature close
calling, "Live, live,
oh please, live, live, live."

And in the city
on Christmas eve
a friend dies
over the telephone,
while my daughter's

toys are painted. For
an hour we dropped
our brushes.

Weeks before I had
caught her falling body
after seeing sycamores
with no green out her
window; she said
when she was back in bed,
"I missed all of
October and November. . . ."
We weaved from side to side
down the hall
to watch the ocean over
a bowl of fruit on her
kitchen table.

She had whispered to me
in October, "We all
live to be loved. . . ."
and we wept but she
forgot October and we
listened
to cars pull away, dogs
bark, while her older
son told the younger
he was not invited
to the birth
day party.
He cried
while his pants
were changed.

"Of course you can go
to the party," he was gently
told.

On New Year's eve
in the cold final
snow of January
I sucked in air and
fell back into the
shocking softness.
The white of snow
reminded me of bones
and a voice in my head
shouted, "Live,
we have no right
to let even a
particle die so
live even as they
push you to the wall
even as they spit out your name
behind wild
accusations, live even
with anger, even
if the sycamores seem tired,
spit back,
rock, press everything close
the skin, the flesh
that can so quickly turn yellow and
thin," I put my face
in the snow, and snow sang back
live, oh please, live, live, live, live
and
I wept,
yes.

Repairs

Repairs.
patches.
sand and
paint and
a little thread,
a graft,
a little
rest, a bit of
sun, some good
food, a new pot,
a new dress,
a good soaking,
dusting,
a shine,
a little oil,
a good run, a breath of
fresh
air, one half
boric acid and one
half golden seal,
homeopathy,
constant pressure
to
the area of pain,
fresh vegetables and
natural foods,
Yoga, life
energy, medi-
tation,
touching, touch

your lips to the
genitals,
your fingers to
the skin,
brush your hair
on the belly,
and sing,
turn over
the earth, clip
the branches, and weep
to make it better, make
it better,
make it better.

Poem in the Form of a Letter

Dear who
can I address this to
there is no way
to speak
anymore . . . even the forms are wrong, one word
after the other, sounding like
sounding like, sounding like
whatever it is that is
stopping us from
being whatever, the problem is
violence, or not violence, or fear,
or not fear enough. I wrote a short
poem the night the choppers were out
in Berkeley, it ended, "if anything
happens to you
I will kill everybody." And this morning,
I thought of a poem that would begin,
"I have failed
as an activist."
Perhaps it's just me
who lacks the proper
organizational talents for
getting everyone
together to do something but the truth is
I haven't the heart for it
anymore. I feel defeated.

I stand with my hands in my
pockets, wearing overalls
but with no work to do,

staring into the green leaves of
a begonia that is going dormant,
and needs no water, nothing.

Everyone asks me what I'm doing.
Well, today I went to buy a goldfish,
to live with the other goldfish
in the bowl on our kitchen table.
My daughter named the fish after
two friends who
live together.

Last night I drove twenty miles to
school to attend a class that was
given the night before last.
The classroom was empty. I
wandered past the open doors
and seeing row upon row of bored faces
decided to go home.

Today I waited for the mail,
telephoned another school who said,
"We have three people a day
come in looking for work."
I am writing a short novel that no one
will want to publish.

I feel like a silo full of grain
that has been dumped in the ocean
when there are people
starving,
all over the
world.

If I were to turn myself into a
photograph
ten years from now
I might
understand
where this is all leading to,
is there
something
sacred about life? I ask,
and reach hesitantly
for what I know for sure
to those I love I still whisper
don't die.

Letter to the Revolution

Revolution,
Damn you, I have
a thousand accusations to make:
you failed to save the life
of George Jackson, and you
failed to make yourself
pure.   Like a dumb animal
you have turned on your best
friends. You pretended great
change, in the name of the children
of the bourgeois while the
children of the poor
still suffer. You make promises,
which you have not kept.
You have taken more pleasure in
slander than in understanding and
if you have not lied
you have participated in illusions.
You failed in the worst moments
to bring even a shred of hope
and at the best times, to give
love. You have taken time
and blood freely but
if you have given anything
it is secret.
You have made friends into enemies,
parents to strangers and children
afraid. You boast frequently
about your accomplishments
always elsewhere, and you speak

of humanity, but your first
movements are always
cruel. Revolution,
I find your presence
everywhere, but nowhere
do I find your heart.

An Answer to a Man's Question,
"What Can I Do About Women's Liberation?"

Wear a dress.

Wear a dress that you made yourself, or bought in a dress
    store.

Wear a dress and underneath the dress wear elastic,
    around

your hips, and underneath your nipples.

Wear a dress and underneath the dress wear a sanitary
    napkin.

Wear a dress and wear sling-back, high-heeled shoes.

Wear a dress, with elastic and a sanitary napkin under-
    neath,

and sling-back shoes on your feet, and walk down
    Telegraph Avenue.

Wear a dress, with elastic and a sanitary napkin and
    sling-

back shoes on Telegraph Avenue and try to run.

Find a man.

Find a nice man who you would like to ask you for a
    date.

Find a nice man who *will* ask you for a date.

Keep your dress on.

Ask the nice man who asks you for a date to come to
    dinner.

Cook the nice man a nice dinner so the dinner is ready
    before

he comes and your dress is nice and clean and wear a
    smile.

Tell the nice man you're a virgin, or you don't have

birth control, or you would like to get to know him
better.

Keep your dress on.

Go to the movies by yourself.

Find a job.

Iron your dress.

Wear your ironed dress and promise the boss you won't
get

pregnant (which in your case is predictable) and you
like to

type, and be sincere and wear your smile.

Find a job or get on welfare.

Borrow a child and get on welfare.

Borrow a child and stay in the house all day with the
child,

or go to the public park with the child, and take the child

to the welfare office and cry and say your man left you
and

be humble and wear your dress and your smile, and don't
talk

back, keep your dress on, cook more nice dinners, stay

away from Telegraph Avenue, and still, you won't
know the

half of it, not in a million years.

II

FAMILY
(1967–1976)

Grenadine

The movies, she told me
ruined my life.
We were sitting there
drinking bourbon and soda
flavored by grenadine.
I in the leather chair
that engulfed me
carrying me back,
on the television
a late movie
we weren't watching,
its noise took up our silences.
She was fat from all her drinking
and her eyes darted
unfocused about the room
her voice jumped from deep
to high laughter.
Really, she said,
No kidding, she said,
I mean that. The
movies, she said,
curling her lip
and looking meanly
at George Sanders
on the TV.
"They," she said,
pointing and accusing,
"tell you things about life
that aren't true."
She sat

staring a long time
trying to focus on my eyes.
"Hello, sweetie," she said
and smiled at me
like a cockeyed hula dancer
from inside a ukulele.
She put her glass embellished with splashes of
gold on the metal TV tray
her feet on the leather stool.
She had it fixed
so she never had to move.
"Your father," she said,
"he was a good man,
do you know why
we di-
vorced?"
"No."
I stared at the
grenadine in my bourbon.
"Because of the movies,"
she said.
I blinked past her eyes
heaved in the leather chair
trying to upright myself
trying to refill my glass,
the television
busily selling cars,
my stepfather snoring on
the couch
like a giant vacuum cleaner.
She laughed
a high-pitched laugh and tried
her very best

to stare right at me.
"We would go to the movies
your father and I."
I nodded at her.
"And I'd come out
being Carole Lombard,
only he refused
to be Humphrey Bogart."
We stared at each other,
the television
sticking to the sides of our faces
George Sanders pretending to be
evil pretending to be good
being unmasked by
Rosalind Russell pretending
to be a lady reporter
pretending in real life
all she really wanted was
a home and family she said
to *Ladies Home Journal* reporter but
job of acting and stardom
thrust upon her
never found right man.
"All the myths," my mother
said. "I saw a movie
about, about
they made me think," she said,
running off with another man
would be African jungle
beautiful in dark green
Don Ameche canoeing to
palace in wilderness
speaking mad poetry

of love
absolute lusty
freedomofitall
glorious spirit of man
kissing
in white bow tie
and unconquerable
white orchid
maraschino cherry red lips
she said
they made it look so glamorous
drinking her grenadine bourbon
and fell asleep,
my stepfather snoring
on the couch
while the dog
whined outside the screen door
to be let in.

Grandmother

After so long
she died.
Eighty years old,
they said,
"She had a long life;
she didn't suffer
when she went."
That's not the point.
But what is?
We should have all got
together
after all of these years,
strung out all over
the state, but she
would not have
a funeral and was
burned. She was
my Grandmother,
held me on her lap
when I was young.
I wept on her
breast and combed her
white hair, and
loved her for the way
her arms knew
my pain. She taught me
to read, and brush my
teeth, iron my clothes,
scramble eggs,
spread jam on bread,
clean up crumbs from

all the tables, grind
meat, stifle laughs,
grit my teeth, say the
right thing,
shake hands, watch to see
if my slip was hanging, to
put my hair in a french roll
wear mascara and
use a lip brush,
file my nails, bathe in
oil. She saved little things for me.
Her things, she'd say,
"My things, let me show
you my things; don't
let a stranger
who doesn't know
their value, touch
my things." The crystal
polar bears, the
rose plates,
the chair we could never
sit in. I don't want them.
I want
my Grandmother
so we might
do what we
should have done
in life,
sit down together
drunk or tired and
worn down or crazy with
ecstasy, so we might
sit down together
and sing out our grief.

Grandfather

He leaned forward
the emphysema like silver
in his lungs,
"Those niggers,"
he coughed and
confided in me,
"they're all savages."
Dear Grandpa
of the carnation flower garden
and polished Dodge,
I remember you
fingering your nitrate ties,
pulling cigarettes from
leather cases, you
whispered about
"those niggers,"
and stood behind the
swinging door
as women brought you
plates of roast beef
and shined the kitchen floor.
He's in the cemetery
now, this old man
who liked to wink at me
and slip me shots of bourbon
behind my Grandma's back.
He played the mandolin and
told us stories—his
mind was full of
crime. The seven little
indians, the lady

in the lake. His argot
came from selling cars,
so much
was traded in, and now
there are more highways to
travel nowhere by. But
nothing
works against death; the savages
in his heart are coming home,
and they are his children
more savage than ever he dreamed

This Enemy

I hate
this enemy
who has killed
most of my family
half of everyone I've loved
part of me.
I meet
it walking
in the face of a
man hurrying.
He is too
busy to
see, his eyes
blank.
She,
my Grandmother,
kept a diary
where she wrote
each day,
what was bought &
sold, got done,
said and promised.
I looked at
her things
when she was
dead. She was
a good child
even when no one
came to see her being good.
The bureau was clean and

all the family portraits
neatly framed.
Grandfather, who had died,
posing in his handsome youth,
his pocketknife placed tenderly
by his likeness.
What was this gesture when
his life was every day, she made clear,
a burden to her?
We build buildings
and nothing more.
The steady hammering
of progress is so loud
the thought I had
which caused a great rush down my belly through
my heart,
a softness letting in the sweet blue
sky was forgotten.
This enemy
grew up with me.

Archaeology of a Lost Woman: Fragments

i

A book stained with
years of use:
The Joy of Cooking.

The pieces
of a mixing bowl
taken apart
displayed
by her Granddaughter
as sculpture.

Her sweater, knitted
magenta wool.

Her hands, long
misshapen fingers spotted
brown.

The old needles
the old patterns.

Her voice still saying,
"If my face is stern
it is because it has grown
to look that way
despite me."

ii

A walk through a
museum, women
in photography, a

picture of
an ironing board, an
iron before a window,
a shadow cast in the
natural light.

iii

She remembers holding her hand,
her Grandmother's secret
knowledge,
the two boarding the trolley, the
yearly trip downtown,
the school clothes, the
joy that day, the
laughter between the two, the
promise of something sweet at
home, the old woman, her
promise.

She remembers longing
to walk
the light out there
beautiful
through the open door.

She remembers words
to her daughter, "Hurry,
be
careful, don't
spill
over me." She remembers

her Grandmother's voice
the hardness, then,
the weariness.

iv

Words in an old diary
Sunday, March 23, 1958

> Home all day. Black clouds. Quite
> dark at times. However I did laundry
> so I could go out in the morning. Dried
> in and out. Quite a breeze. Washed doll
> clothes. Must make her a footstool.
> Finally made Ernie's fudge. Fried the
> chicken in the pan and was moist
> and very good. Rest and after went
> to sleep. Bed at 9:30. Read a bit.
> . . . Awake for ages. Too tired to get
> up or read. Just tossed and turned . . .

v

In the museum
photographs of women
their hands over their mouths,

women standing
side by side
not touching
the lassitude of
unloving
in them,

etching of a woman alone
called waiting,

woman and child
asleep in the railway station,

a face staring into the lens
"I am what I am
broken, you will
see that in time."

a woman passed through
slavery, letting her eyes
blaze, "My body
carries this pain
like an emblem.
I do not apologize.
I survive."

vi

Child's memories
dolls cut
from cloth
new faces threaded
each year

candy distilled
to hardness
over the fire

an old drawing sent
through the mail,
"I love you
Mommy,"
Archaeology

the waters
of sleep we had
no time to swim

My cries at night

the ache in my knees
her old stockings
around my legs

my daughter's nightmare
my arms around her, my
face pleading, "Don't
wake up again."

Her tenderness, my desire to
please breaking like vases
along the lines of
old faults,

the flower I gave her
she did not believe would bloom

ink spilled on the satin
bed covers, the furies
if you don't
welling inside her
stop crying
the darkness of my room
if you don't
stop

vii

waters of sleep
flowers blooming
my daughter brought forward
like a sweet

My Grandmother
floats in my dreams
we sleep

like sisters in
the peach-colored room
where I slept
as a child, and in
my womb I feed
the Great Grandchild
she always wanted.

Archaeos, the
shards of
disbelief
the last words never
spoken how I
loved you old
complaining woman, the
pieces, the stairs
were slippery,
and she slipped,
broken one more
time,
pieces
her mixing bowl on my
the silver bell she saved for me

viii

Do you know
I ask her
calling through time
I write this
with your pen?

ix

Becky, my
daughter rocks
in my Great Grand
mother's chair, that
chair,
I tell her,
sat
in my Grandmother's house
in the peach-colored room,
don't sit too hard
it's been
years.

x

Night, darkness, the healing
sleep, the vessel fused
once more,
one of us writes in her journal
A tiredness has left me
A heaviness
one of us whispers
O world is this what you were
and tenderness,
Grandmother
your tenderness sings
in my skin.

III

THE TIREDNESS CYCLE

(1973–1974)

Tiredness

Tiredness licks
at my heels
an old
dog
walking across
the patio;
the belly is gone,
the hair
faded.
I have traveled
from
patio to patio, pool to pool
dipping my feet
in various seas
(Aegean, Atlantic, Pacific)
waking each
time as if
now I would
stay awake
and my feet
would not
doggedly shuffle
in the same circle
looking at
each point
for the sunlight
on the water.
Tiredness,
I give in to you.
I am making a

house for you.
I will love you
like an old dress
become worn and soft.
I will smile on you
with your hair
turning dull and old.
I will welcome your aching and
your half-open eyes
because tiredness at least
you
have always been
faithful.

Always

I am trying to
salvage the day again
that started at quarter to nine.
I was safe in the kitchen till noon
and I knew even then
I shouldn't have left.
Upstairs closets yawn half-
written notes to me
while I sit
in black underpants
deciding what to wear.
The sunlight is saying
go out the door but
where?
Should I stay in all day
and cry
or should I try
to change the look of things
inside?

In my mind I
imagine a group of women
concerned about me—
they make a thousand
suggestions and then
one by one
leave.
I sit with all their
suggestions,
I tell them

what is the use,
I hold them, break
down, I murmur,
breakdown, I hold them
close.

Were you always like this? they
ask me
as they
swiftly move
away.
Yes, yes
I freeze, I am
freezing, yes,
I am standing
stock still, I
am always like this,
I have always been
and I always will.

And always the house is the same.
The window is standing open,
the door is shut,
it is quarter to one,
the morning is done—
the day has more than begun.

Serious

I am tired
I have read my poetry
which made my friends laugh.
Alice tells me,
"You'll be the
Lenny Bruce of the
Woman's Movement."
And just when I
thought I was
getting serious.
I was having lunch
every day
in the middle of the day.
I was serious
with calendars and
carbon
copies of letters and
file boxes.
I have a muffler on
my car and at night
I brush my daughter's teeth.

My life takes on
a recognizable shape
I arrive places at
predictable hours and
on vacations
I dive into the sea.

Last Saturday
I wandered from room to room
cleaning and
weeping: Things are
always the same.
I wrote a poem called "Always."
This Saturday
I rocked in my clean
living room
read someone else's poems and thought:

There is a time for everything
a time to clean
a time to weep
a time to read
a time to brush your daughter's teeth
and replace them each
with a dime.

The doorbell rang
and I let in a friend
who pointed
out her
period on my kitchen
calendar
and bled into my toilet bowl.

In the Museum I said
is a painting
of menstrual blood.
And in another gallery
photographs
of faces all over

the world
some the faces of the dead
now
all
with the same expectant
expression.

I remember Lenny Bruce
said the Jews
and all oppressed people
sing, dance and tell jokes
to charm the boss
so they can get away with
lighter sentences.

Lenny Bruce is more dead than God now
but we
have a moving
picture of him.

And day after day
I sense
I am getting away with it
        getting away
and wait to find out
with what.

I have succeeded in charming
myself away
from my own urgency:
in the dark
some are
drinking themselves to death

and some are so
nervous they never
sit down.
I am serious,
I am laughing,
I dwell
on the line.

Chile

My daughter pleads with me
for the life of our goldfish
souring in a tank
of ancient water,
"I want them
to
live," she
says.   Late at night
I pass the green tank
still full of guilt.
I have chosen
in the hierarchy of my life
to go to work,
to shop, to cook, to
write these words
before saving the fish;
choices surround me.
Nothing is ever right.
Every breathing space
asks for help;
dust multiplies in the
                hallway;
lecture notes fly away
through windows which
need glass and paint
and in the back of my mind
somewhere
is a woman
who weeps
for Chile

and shudders at the
executions.
All along she
has been
pondering the social order
and her
worried thoughts
slow
my
every movement.

This Is the Story of the Day in the Life of a Woman Trying

This is the story of the day in the life of a woman trying
to be a writer and her child got sick. And in the midst of
writing this story someone called her on the telephone.
And, of course, despite her original hostile reaction to the
ring of the telephone, she got interested in the conversation
which was about teaching writing in a women's prison,
for no pay of course, and she would have done it if it
weren't for the babysitting and the lack of money for the
plane fare, and then she hung up the phone and looked
at her typewriter, and for an instant swore her original
sentence was not there. But after a while she found it. Then
she began again, but in the midst of the second sentence,
a man telephoned wanting to speak to the woman she
shares her house with, who was not available to speak on
the telephone, and by the time she got back to her type-
writer she began to worry about her sick daughter down-
stairs. And why hadn't the agency for babysitters called back
and why hadn't the department for health called back
because she was looking for a day sitter and a night sitter,
one so she could teach the next day and one so she could
read her poetry. And she was hoping that the people who
had asked her to read poetry would pay for the babysitter
since the next evening after that would be a meeting of
teachers whom she wanted to meet and she could not afford
two nights of babysitters let alone one, actually. This was
the second day her child was sick and the second day she
tried to write (she had been trying to be a writer for years)
but she failed entirely the first day because of going to the
market to buy Vitamin C and to the toy store to buy cutouts

and crayons, and making soup from the chicken carcass that
had been picked nearly clean to make sandwiches for
lunch, and watering the plants, sending in the mortgage
check and other checks to cover that check to the bank,
and feeling tired, wishing she had a job, talking on the tele-
phone, and putting out newspaper and glue and scissors
on the kitchen table for her tired, bored child and squint-
ing her eyes at the clock waiting for *Sesame Street* to begin
again. Suddenly, after she went upstairs to her bedroom
with a book, having given up writing as impossible, it was
time to cook dinner. But she woke up on the second day
with the day before as a lesson in her mind. Then an old
friend called who had come to town whom she was eager
to see and she said, "Yes, I'm home with a sick child," and
they spent the morning talking. She was writing poetry and
teaching she said. He had written four books he
said. Her daughter showed him her red and blue and
orange colored pictures. She wished he didn't have to leave
so early, she thought but didn't say, and went back to pick
up tissue paper off the floor and fix lunch for her and her
child and begin telephoning for babysitters because she
knew she had to teach the next day. And the truth was,
if she did not have a sick child to care for, she was
not sure she could write anyway because the kitchen was
still there needing cleaning, the garden there needing
weeding and watering, the living room needing curtains,
the couch needing pillows, a stack of mail needing answers
(for instance if she didn't call the woman who had lived
in her house the month before about the phone bill soon,
she would lose a lot of money). All besides, she had
nothing to write. She had had fine thoughts for writing the
night before but in the morning they took on a sickly
complexion. And anyway, she had begun to think her life

trivial and so it was, and she was tired writing the same words, or different words about the same situation, the situation or situations being that she was tired, tired of trying to write, tired of poverty or almost poverty or fear of poverty, tired of the kitchen being dirty, tired of having no lover. She was amazed that she had gotten herself dressed, actually, with thoughts like these, and caught herself saying maybe I should take a trip when she realized she had just come back from a trip and had wanted to be home so much she came back early. And even in the writing of this she thought I have written all this before and went downstairs to find her daughter had still not eaten a peanut butter sandwich and she wondered to herself what keeps that child alive?

A Piece of Writing About the Parts

This is a piece of writing about the parts that die.
Which parts have died or will die I cannot clearly name.
Their deaths occur before
the shapes of their identities
still infantile, still motionless and curled
become clear.
One feels only a vague lack and remembers
the causes of death more than
what actually died.
One of the causes certainly is death
itself, the deaths say for instance
the death of the father (or it might have
been a mother) and with this dies
the lack of awareness of death that
makes the child's life
youthful.
But some of the parts die
a slower death;
a certain eagerness of
mind for instance seems to be subject to
a permanent sleep
and the causes of this moribund process
are woven into every minute during
which circumstances appear to be
overwhelming and the subject perhaps
turns her back and
says, "All this is making me tired."
And some of the parts struggle and
refuse to die but weaken,
the voice becoming hoarse

and even a bit cynical
for instance
considering one human
being's compatibility with another.
And some
one is glad to see buried and done
with as when the subject learns
for the final time
that expectations are dangerous
that opening one's mouth
is foolish
that going forwards or backwards
is a reciprocal process.
And some
one forgets ever existed
except as perceived
in the eloquence or grace of others
and that may be perceived with anger or even
jealousy for
the question is, is it true
that one is either born to jump high
or one is not,
that one holds genius in her hands
at birth, or
one does not,
that birth
and not
the lack or presence
of food and mother and father
and grants-in-aid or
state-supported schools
or central heating
or books on shelves or curtains on windows

or laudatory remarks
or degrees in frames
or accidental falls from carriages or private
rooms, or paint brushes or
ink or a reading public or space or time or
folded laundry or letters in boxes
but birth alone is the spark
that determines every baby
every child, every youthful or aged
step toward a destiny
written only for geniuses and that true genius
evades every accidental, fortuitous or
systematic detail of life?
Or is genius instead
like all the other
parts that can die
before naming,
a substance
variable in shape and color
altered by circumstance and
perishable.

IV

NEW POEMS
(1973–1976)

The Great Mother

I was walking in
Tilden Park
ready to
throw myself
down a ravine
when suddenly
from a helicopter
parachuted
The Great Mother.
"Hello," she said,
and immediately
surrounded me in an aura
of light and comfort. "Never,
again," she sang,
"will you walk
alone and in anguish."
I was
thrilled and
about to express my
amazement when
suddenly she backed off
and put up her hand,
"Don't ask!"—she smiled—
"I know your every thought
before you even
open your mouth. You
wanted to know
why didn't I come before?"
I opened my mouth to say

no, but
before I could speak she
answered.
"In wanting to
throw yourself
down the ravine
your anguish was so
deep that
suddenly I knew you
truly needed me," she said, and
her hair fanned out
green the color
of the oak
tree growing from the ravine, so
I wanted to say "Yes, but
there were other times I've
wanted to throw myself down
other ravines,"
still, afraid to offend her,
I remained silent.
"I know what your
silence means,"
she said.
"You are asking if
I *am* the Great Mother
all powerful
able to answer all
cries of anguish in all
parks, private and public places
why did I let the anguish
exist in the first place?"
I said nothing.
"A good question," she said.

"And you must already know
  the answer, it is"—she
  gestured gracefully with
  a swanlike movement of her enormous
  sari billowing in the wind—
"One of my mysteries."
  I gaped.
"You must also wonder,"
  she went on,
  looking now to the skies,
"If I am so
  kind
  just
  and all-knowing
  hearing every cry
  how can I answer
  the 11 million eight hundred
  and forty-three
  cries of truly significant
  anguish,
  that come to me
  every five minutes,
  on a statistical average."
  I shrugged my shoulders.
"Because," she said,
"*that* is another mystery."
  She went on.
"The Great Mother
  takes a multitude
  of shapes in a multitude
  of places
  breast, womb, heart
  chicken soup, Red Cross

nurse, milk of human
kindness, security blanket,
these are but
signs of my eternal
hovering presence
but only do I
materialize when
a true seeker . . ."
"Just a moment," I
said
beginning
to catch my breath
but then she
began to fade.
"I am," I said,
and then she disappeared al-
together
and I whispered to
myself filled with
awe, "I am
an
atheist."

For M. M.

I love you
I love you for your height
for your clogged up nose
for the smirk your mouth makes
for the books on your night table
for the scraps of newspaper in your purse
I love you
you
for your stories about 42nd street
told in the right accent
for your poverty program dance
for your falconetti eyes
for your sugar twin box
for your hands which fan outward palms up
to punctuate the obvious
and for your raised eyebrows
for your velvet jumpsuit
for your low ceiling
for your list of projects
for your smoking
for your smoking someone else's cigarettes
for your love for
this one who is heroic with three
children and that one who has
will with one
for your love
and your eyebrows rising again
and you saying the obvious
which was not so obvious
until you said it

and the beansprouts growing in your window
and your hyperventilating breath
becoming kundalini energy in one
magic instant
and your voice that snarls
or almost
disappears
when you talk about functioning
instead of
instead of
and all your film festivals
and your film festival mind
and I love, and I love and I am terribly
afraid of that sashay step
you take quickly away
into your small hot-plate place
into your windbreaker sweater
into your trip to Paris
into your scheduled schedule and into
your self
your self
your self.

Clothing

Returning from the
I would have gone with
no shirt to the
I got the job at the
job interview
taking off my silk shirt
I thought
my velvet pants
my gold necklace
to make me look like
an English teacher
welcoming my white breasts
Nobel Laureate
islands in tan skin and
home I stared
soul broken at the
out our window
dusty leaves of a
plum tree saying
I would have
breasted the truth
I'd wished
I'd said it all
or even lived the
dream, I
once walked out
naked to school
the art,
the artist,
the artifice,

the artificial
dream was
dressed and fed and fat and
happy expecting a pay
check, the hedge
trimmed, jaws together
and no
thing extra
ordinary
here not even
unplanned
orgasm,
vagina and mouth and
eyes and ears
stuffed
and ready to
go
if you
want to
know
she says
why I'm bitter
I've got a
clean house
and what
more could
you ask
the tissue
of my
dream
contracts and joy
is a steady
lie the

flat voice calls
before
slamming the door.
Alone
the house
echoes to me
and for an instant I
am gone—
only my clothes
remain.

Pieces

You said you were
fat and stupid
and clumsy and I
was astonished.
You stayed inside
your body
all year.
I looked for you, you
answered none
of my calls.

I saw you in glimpses
stumbling
over the pieces you left
scattered about the room.
I did not complain
of your housekeeping,
only kept
what I could find,
your hand
settling on my breast, your
tongue lying, your
toes
looking dead, though the vein
in your neck
was beating.

I put the pieces in a
sack; I spoke
through the opening

but heard back
only weeping. I
abandoned your
parts, I denied
you, discovering
you
vanishing as I
called out
from memory,
"You were not fat,"
I remembered,
you were not stupid,
you were never
clumsy.

The Pain Driven Through Me

The pain driven through me
out of me around me I am
numb you have come
and gone and so
has the love I had for you
mocking me
with the coldest hands
that lay themselves on
my head praying for
clarity and I look
out on the clearest day
seeing the mountains
the edges of the sea, the
sea, the brightness of a
green house I have not
seen before in this cold
sharp air, we are reminded
by the dying
of history and how our lives
form shapes together which we
together might
alter and I tell you
my life is wedded to
events like a Siamese twin
the tissue white and thin
something in this flat almost
tearless memory of pain
wanting to cling to bombsites
to cradle myself in the
extermination or threat of

extermination, mirrors
not of tenderness
but of the lack of
tenderness my body
understands rebelling
now against all half
promises, the pain
like a spore bursting
in my lung, my body
refusing to, trying
against the weight of
my rage with which I
tear it daily bit by bit
away from that memory
of arms, of hands,
of shaking like a newborn thing, while
my skin whispered *this*
should be and the clear earth
exquisite cries outside the window
behind me.

The Woman Who Swims in Her Tears

The woman who swims in her tears
the woman who dives down deep
              in her weeping, the
woman who floats downstream in
              her grieving, the
woman who lives in the depths of her
                  crying
                  of her aching
                  of her holding
                    herself
        with her own arms
        and rocking, the
woman who has no mother, the
woman who mothers,
the woman filled with love
who looks at herself
through a closed glass window
and wonders why she cannot touch.

The woman
who slept beside the body of one
other woman weeping,
the women who wept.
the women whose tears wet
      each other's hair
the woman who wrapped her legs
      around another woman's thigh
    and said I am afraid.
the woman who put her head
      in the

place between the shoulder and breast
of the other woman and
said, "Am I wrong?"
the women who wept together
the women who pressed
their faces together
their hands together
their eyes together
their thighs together
who pressed into each other
who cried together
who cried
who cried out
who cried out joy
the women who
cried out joy
together.

Her Sadness Runs Beside Her Like a Horse

Her sadness runs beside her
like a horse
        now she is
riding the horse of her sadness
      riding, riding, riding.
Does she wear a hat?
No.
That is her hair you see
which the wind
whips into her eyes.
Does she cry?
No.
The wind cries
the horse cries
she grips his body
with her thighs,
they are changing
direction
riding into the sun.
Who
knows the way,
the woman or the
horse-of-her-sadness?
Her thighs know
his body knows.
Will they ever stop
riding?
What?
Look,
now they have

traveled
below the horizon.
Now we can
only wait.
Will they
ever
return?
But they are
here now.
Where?
Listen,
don't you hear
them
galloping
under this earth?

The Song of the Woman with Her Parts Coming Out

I am bleeding
the blood seeps in red
circles on the white
white of my sheet,
my vagina
is opening, opening
closing and opening;
wet, wet,
my nipples turn rose and hard
my breasts swell against my arms
my arms float out
like anemones
my feet slide on the wooden
floor,
dancing, they are dancing, I sing,
my tongue slips from my mouth
and my mind
imagines a
clitoris
I am the woman
I am the woman
with her parts coming out
with her parts coming out.

The song of the woman with
the top of her head ripping off, with
the top of her head ripping off
and she flies out
and she flies out

and her flesh flies out
and her nose rubs against her ass,
and her eyes love ass
and her cunt
swells and sucks and waves,
and the words spring from her mind
like Fourth of July rockets,
and the words too come out,
lesbian, lesbian, lesbian, pee, pee, pee, pee, cunt, vagina,
dyke, sex, sex, sex, sex, sweat, tongue, lick, suck, sweet,
sweet, sweet, suck
and the other words march out too,
the words,
P's and Q's
the word
nice,
the word
virginity,
the word
mother,
mother goodness mother nice good goodness good good
        should
should be good be mother be nice good
the word
pure
the word
lascivious
the word
modest
the word
no
the word
no

the word
no
and the woman
the woman
the woman
with her
parts coming out
never stopped
never stopped
even to
say yes,
but only
flew with
her words
with her words
with her words
with her parts
with her parts
coming
with her parts
            coming
            coming
            coming
            out.

A Woman Defending Herself
Examines Her Own Character
Witness

QUESTION: Who am I?

ANSWER: You are a woman.

Q. How did you come to meet me?

A. I came to meet you through my own pain and suffering.

Q. How long have you known me?

A. I feel I have known you since my first conscious moment.

Q. But how long really?

A. Since my first conscious moment—for four years.

Q. How old are you?

A. Thirty-one years old.

Q. Will you explain this to the court?

A. I was not conscious until I met you through my own pain and suffering.

Q. And this was four years ago?

A. This was four years ago.

Q. Why did it take you so long?

A. I was told lies.

Q. What kind of lies?

A. Lies about you.

Q. Who told you these lies?

A. Everyone. Most only repeating the lies they were told.

Q. And how did you find out the truth?

A. I did not. I only stopped hearing lies.

Q. No more lies were told?

A. Oh no. The lies are still told, but I stopped hearing them.

Q. Why?

A. My own feelings became too loud.

Q. You could not silence your own feelings any longer?

A. That is correct.

Q. What kind of woman am I?

A. You are a woman I recognize.

Q. How do you recognize me?

A. You are a woman who is angry.

You are a woman who is tired.

You are a woman who receives letters from her children.

You are a woman who was raped.

You are a woman who speaks too loudly.

You are a woman without a degree.

You are a woman with short hair.

You are a woman who takes her mother home from the hospital.

You are a woman who reads books about other women.

You are a woman whose light is on at four in the morning.

You are a woman who wants more.

You are a woman who stopped in her tracks.

You are a woman who will not say please.

You are a woman who has had enough.

You are a woman clear in your rage.

And they are afraid of you

I know

they are afraid of you.

Q. This last must be stricken from the record as the witness does not know it for a fact.

A. I know it for a fact that they are afraid of you.

Q. How do you know?

A. Because of the way they tell lies about you.

Q. If you go on with this line you will be instructed to remain silent.

A. And that is what they require of us.

Mother and Child

Mother
I write home
I am alone and
give me my
body back.

(She drank
she drank and
did not feed me
I was the child at home.)

You have given me disease:
All
the old
areas of infection reopen themselves:
my breath
rasps,
my head
is an
argument,
my blood ebbs, you
and your damned Irish genes
did this to me.

I pretend
someone else
cares for me,
catches my
falling body,
cradles my
aching head,

cries when my fever rises
in alarm.

And meanwhile
mother
from my dying bed
I have
finished you, you are
not even a
spot upon the sheet,
you are gamma rayed
clean gone.

You are not
absent anymore
you
never were.

And your child
is the driven snow, she
is innocent of
all action, the
articulate say victim,
a word
she neither speaks nor
knows.

She is buried. She is only
bone, polished clean and white
as if with
agonized toil
a shrunken jeweler
crouched inside

her box
tumbling her body
by hand but
she was alone.

She was alone, but
her casket
was glass. And when she
cried she turned
her body
in shame
to the earth, and
turning and turning
wore her
body away.

Now
in my dreams
the mother who never was
finds the bones of her child
and says,
"How we have both suffered."

Now the
child opens the
box which becomes
a mirror. She stares at her
bony self
and does not
look away.

Field

To rage I
gravitate in
the field of
your fear.

We see by
force of
circumstance:
I listed
all you had
and now
I list your
lacks.
Loving
is not seeing
but the lover
sees.

She turns from
truth to truth.
She moves across a
room ̄ and in this
distance
breathes, re-
covers her-
self, names
her discomfort
which had
needled

her like a
drug.

    You are two
    not I.
    The one I love
    the other
    belies

        all we know together
        all we have barely seen
        delicate as the line between
        the air and your face

    How can you ask me to love her?
    This blunt
    one, this denier?

She is your sister
swollen, blunted,
blue,
and she is frightened of me
this dumb
woman, this
buried
force
in you.

Waiting for Truth

Their bodies lined up against the walls
waiting for truth, my
words thread the room
like fishing line,
"She put
she put her head in an oven
she put her head in an
oven,"
I stutter,
my words enter space and I
slide down the line
terrified, where are we
going?
Their bodies wait for information.
"There are places I have been," I
want to tell them.
The book behind me reads:
        "Sylvia Plath's range of technical resources . . ."
"There are places I have been," I
want to say, my body
all night sleeping,
did I dream
running in Harlem
dream the markets of the
poor,
was someone diseased, was the disease
spreading? Did I dream
an escape? Was I safe in a
classroom, sitting close
to a friend, sighing relief,

writing the movie script,
telling where I had been,
was I singing?
Did they say my name?
That I was supposed to write words
on the chalkboard, I
was supposed to address and I
stuttered,
"What I have seen
the places I have been and I
promised everyone there
I would speak only of *them*:
the one who sat in a corner for a week,
the one whose breasts ran dry,"
And the book read,
      "Sylvia Plath
      Sylvia Plath's range of
      technical resources was narrower
      than Robert Lowell's,"* and I
stuttered:
"The one whose lovers
were frightened by her
children, the one who
wished her children,"
      "Narrower than Robert Lowell's and so,
      apparently, was her capacity"

---

* The line "Sylvia Plath's range of technical resources was narrower than Robert Lowell's and so, apparently, was her capacity for intellectual objectivity" is from the essay "Sylvia Plath and Confessional Poetry," by M. L. Rosenthal, which appears in *The Art of Sylvia Plath*, Charles Newman, ed. (Indiana U. Press, 1971).

her children would be
          "for intellectual objectivity."
would be still.
Sylvia Plath's range of
technical resources
she put her
was narrower
head in an
there are places I have been
Everyone on the street was diseased.
There are places you have been.
Trying to speak
the script
claiming my mind, was it
a dream
or did I live, "range of
technical."
Their bodies in transformation.
She put her head in an
repetition
repetition
is no longer
no longer
interesting in
poetry
he said
but goes on
which one put
her head in an
in life, in
autobiographical detail, gas,
milk, a pair of kids, technical resources, a bottle
of chicken fat, two dinner guests, a box of books,

Achoo IdoAchoo IdoAchoo   I   do
and an interesting sense of rhyme
range of
chattering, "There are places
we have," suddenly the whole
been, there are places, bodies
lined up, the walls, the whole world
suddenly the whole world is making
terrific sense I am chattering,
"Yes," I say to the bus driver, taking me home,
"I am afraid of freeways."
"Yes," I lecture a tree
near the sidewalk, "I am free."
Yes, I am afraid of rats, knives, bullets,
I am, there is, I am there is,
I sing, walking the street,
a fish on the line,
shouting to my feet,
"But I will not be afraid
of voices nor of,"
There are places we
"nor of pieces of paper."
have been.

Breviary

"*Do not let them kill me before you speak to me*
Touch me!
            Behold me!"

MERIDEL LESUEUR
from "Behold Me! Touch Me!"

She is in a white dress
kneeling.
K is for kneeling
in the breviary and
W is for woman.
Women kneel,
small girls wear white dresses
for communion
for communion,
into the bread
the flesh,
the wine and the blood
and the women kneel
for our bread
for our blood.
Do not let them
and the woman
smiles out from her window
offering the picture-taker
a loaf of bread
Do not let them
kill me,
stroking the soft hair
on the head

of her
baby (but we saw the second
picture, the small buttocks
in a pool of blood)
before you speak to me
and the women in white dresses
speak softly to the saints
and the saints answer,
"love befits the man
and fear befits the woman."
the words of the saints spelled
out in gold in the air
sung out by the voices
of small boys, high and light
and pure.
In the other picture one sees a woman crying,
a small old woman, holding on to a younger woman
who is also crying. And under the picture the
cameraman's words tell us that moments later
the daughter was raped and then killed.
The photographer could do nothing. The photo-
graphs were what he did. He was certain he would
be court-martialed or killed for taking them. He
could not stop the massacres. There was nothing
he could do.
Do not let them kill me
before you speak to me
touch me, behold me
And it might have been different if he had
been in his own country or this were not a
war because men act differently in a war.
For I am innocent
and she removed her blouse

she showed her white neck
she opened her empty palms
she kneeled
she wept
she carried a child
she squatted down
she cried
and left a child where she had been
and she whispered to her daughter, stand
she whispered to her daughter, run.
What he wanted or why he did it no one
especially knew. "She's lucky to be alive,"
the police said. She has parts of knives still
in her and knife wounds in her heart, her lung,
her liver, her spleen and her throat. She fought
him off and she lived. She is well except for
some hoarseness. The doctor does not know if her
voice will return to normal.
And the young boys voices sang out
Holy Mary
high and beautiful
Mother of God
with a red heart in her breast
and a red fruit in her mouth
and a slow movement of her thighs
the red tongue of a tiger lily
the red blood of birth
the cry of a child between her thighs
her thighs down hard
birthing the new voice
which is the end of the old voice
blood on the palms of her hands
miraculous and sudden

blood on the sheet that was white
she was in a white dress
kneeling
K is for kneeling
W is for woman
B is for bless, and bread and blood
at the hands of a man,
H is for heathen and healing,
R is for rape, M is for massacre,
W is for woman and the words of the saints,
P is for picture and pool of blood
and for purity and prayer, for prayer and S is for she,
she,
she is in a white dress
kneeling.

Two Thousand Years

1

There you are at the stove again
a woman too intelligent for absolute
paranoia, stirring the cereal
again, is there something that draws you
back and back to this
the light, the plant you must
water, the bacon, the eggs in the pan
you consider five years in this
place, two lunches made in the
ice box, your daughter with
one big tooth crowding the babies
makes blue snakes in the next room,
the cereal is poured in blue
bowls with blue rims,
you have chosen the color
chosen your daughter
chosen the number on the house.

2

You say the
entire world can exist
in one imagination.
And you tell the story
of the sisters over
in your mind
how they longed for the city
how they died in the country
and that not in the city

but somewhere
behind them
not in the country
but behind them, was a shadow, a glimpse, a thought
lying under speech.

3

Always one step ahead of despair
I dreamed last night
the men made plans for the future
your husband and mine
with the correct explosions
underground, they said, we locate caves
and stay there while the holocaust
rages on the surface, then
according to the laws of probability
we will find our way out
in two thousand years.

4

No, I woke up screaming
I would rather die
in the fires.

5

And you wake
to a quick silence
like disaster, like the
moment the pot falling
seems to rest in air
before it

splits in two
and you wonder
is the fire
real?

6

You remind yourself how easily you forget
the mind thinking itself quick recites outlines
and leaves out all the textures,
invents a reason
and is irritated by the wrong details.
The body goes on defending itself
every movement, the boiling of water on
the stove, the pouring of salt in a shaker
a proof of theorems, when suddenly
I remember every moment.

7

Self-preservation in the making of breakfast.
Self-preservation in the cry on waking.
Self-preservation in reason.
Self-preservation in memory.
I remember every moment, I am shocked
at the daily loss.

The Last of the French Movies

i

The images are paling now.
The camera draws away
leaves us
without a screen.
The air
touches
everything.
We are dependent
on the weather
of our souls, no
image
covers us, our
terror is wholly
real, our love the
thinnest thread
what we dread now
as familiar as dreams.
Everything is
what it seems.

ii

And in my dreams
I escape over the ice
in the freezing tundra
I am embraced
by a polar bear
and though I am terrified
the polar bear

looks on me tenderly and
I am in love
for an instant.

      iii

The polar bear embraces me
Cold water embraces me
My bones become ice
My flesh is blue

      iv

I am not image
I am substance:

          when I sigh
          the frost of my breath
          leaves evidence:

I was here.

To this one lone
creature I see
passing, I whisper

lick the ice
drink
know me.

Women

FOR A. R.

We walk in the
old
frozen landscape the
way things are
stuck in our
throats
the grief
still wet
on your face stubborn
like a child with failure
of disbelief

with an eye that
tells and also
sees
what can be

and sorrow all over
your body
the gait moving
moving even in
stillness and in motion
not so predictable
as true
the secret colors
under these leaves of
pain and
loving turning over
in your breath

117

and the vision of joy
under your lid, in a
sudden turn of your
head, your jaw
closed and certain
(because you know)
nothing escapes passion
in this blink
the air leaps—

with it, women, quickness of
spirit, of tongue, the last
lies torn away,
our gestures free at last and
so moving,   they
split us
in two.

Like Water in a Cell There Is a Kind of

Like water in a cell there is a kind of
precision to this chance occurrence
not something given but
coded   like a gene
whose logic
like the logic of a quilt or
tapestry is intricate,
in the past, and there is no
formula for our being together
no simple reason that
suddenly my mind is filled
with your mind like a great
dark night almost filling
the lens of my eye,
the blackness
yielding shape and then
wholly illuminated with
the colors of your
childhood which
become stories and nights at
the dinner table, my child
in your arms until every
gesture turning from your
bones is
familiar, kind, part of
what is called this house
one room lighting up after
another until another
fold is found
holding darkness

which becomes another night and
another layer parts just as
familiarity had begun to
rock us to
sleep
the new
and we are blind again
swimming deep
fold beneath fold
to where only
touch will tell
what this is

what we've never
seen before but felt
and did
we remember
we were here and I
have seen that eye
float in its animal
tenderness she
and I were as close as vision
and light,
and if I
look away, I turn back
to see
you are more
than I can imagine
and in a moment
miracles possess us,
take place
in our ears without
our willing, promise

to enter us, the ear only
an augury, a crystal, miracles
drive us wild, take us
to the door of failure
where a flaw
threads like gold through this
darkness
to the door of final signs, the door
we promised not to enter
and as we enter we
cry.

Here, our bodies suffer
every birth
again the trembling
child held in the
frame floats slowly to
movement finds her
way
free, here
as we turn
in these holdings
strands of silver, gleaming
white and brittleness of
gesture glimmer like
shells telling of
death.

Now, I reach to touch your face
now, I forget all of my life
and all I have forgotten
rushes through me, nothing
is familiar in this

terrifying landscape
every moment
comes back again
and is once again
new.

Nineteen Pieces for Love

1

Lines of poems
surround me

once I wrote
    we talk in cars

once I wrote
    each detail
    must be
    remembered

once I wrote
    our words
    kept from
    the
    air

once I wrote
    everything here is brown

and I wrote
    it is brown I want
    brown at the back of my skull
    on the roof of my mouth

about love
lying
still and deep
    the lake is
at the bottom

brown
in winter.

2

We talk in
cars our
words kept
from the
air.

3

and my body
is a metaphor
it floats
on the surface

each detail

4

there are two
women in
the story
we cannot

tell,

must be

two
women, and
two more women

remembered

5

once I wrote
        I circle the lake and stand
        at each opening, still
        in the stillness, only my eyes
        surprised
        again and again.

and I wrote
        next to me
        in the car
        small shoulders
        weep

6

I am as unsure
as all the rest.

7

We talk of
possessiveness
and I am blessed
to see you
be as
perverse as
me.

8

and I wrote
        in the dark

I distrust
every motion

and once
I will let you go
I will let you go
and not curse you for leaving me
you who are dear to me

and once
I am not a word
I am a substance

9

and felt
let me be
and wrote
a feeling of having
been here
before
and said
open, please
God, and wrote who
is god let me

we have
be
open.

only moments and these
must be

10

remembered.
two women

speaking
of women
while
lines of poetry
surround
them

11

Are you
tired
being the one
who jumps over
edges?

12

edges. I circle
the
let me be
let words
drop into me
tears
     drop into me
hands fall on
the surface of
    my skin
hands

13

lake
and once I wrote
   I have
   no resources
   to fight

what we
unwittingly
might do to
each other.

and I wrote
If I lay
my head on your
breast
will there be
a toll exacted? What will
the payment be?

14

small shoulders
releasing sorrow
and the words
surround us
the words are
all around us
now

15

trying to say
suddenly
what I want
to possess
is not a woman
   not a man
but love
my own
   feeling

16

in the lake
in the water

17

which like magic
sticks
to certain people

18

I am not
let me be
        a word
the words
open let me, the words
drop into me

I am not a word
I am a substance

19

waiting for sureness
when all we have
I wrote
are moments

and these

surprise us,

two women
telling stories
two

women
our words thrown
like stones
            over
the edge

                              (Nineteen Pieces for Love)

        1

It happens quickly
        the body

        2

the face turning to

        3

turning in

    water   water
air

                water
air   water   air

        4

turning to
love
to what was
always

5

light falling in waves
                there
through the blue below

6

flooding my
eyes

7

stillness   in the center
    light amazing the blue
sky   quick with
possibility

8

                              I swim

9

the recognition
felt
as pain

10

old words glisten like
stones at the
and from the edge of the

11

to feel again
what was lost
to see the edge
of what was always

12

of the
depth
        there
water slaps against air
the surface   the body

13

a remembered dream
rises,   speeds
through the waves like
          light like
the dark passage of terror

14

what is
always
there and
unnamed

15

     the dark
no longer
part of

air   part of water of
flesh,

16

full of

power
moving by its own
                         force
to love

17

    with the eyes
    with the mouth
    with the skin

    to see

18

a way through
memory   still
breathing, I put my face
to the air and
then
water, then air, then

19

it is brown I want
at the edge of the lake
brown at the back of my skull
on the roof of my mouth

brown with feeling
I circle the lake
my body a metaphor it
floats on the surface of
and on its surface
the brown trees
the ducks with soft dark
feathers
the sparrows scratching in the
underbrush
a tangle of dried branch root and weed
the dark earth
covered in needles
words like stones in the center
words like circles
of water
I stand
at each opening, still in the
stillness only my eyes
startled again and again
light falling on the still
forms of life
every moment closer
light falling on the stories that have not
been told
to what is missing
light falling
on the moments
we are living.